Collins

Exploring Science

Grade 7

Derek McMonagle

Workbook

Collins

William Collins' dream of knowledge for all began with the publication of his first book in 1819. A self-educated mill worker, he not only enriched millions of lives, but also founded a flourishing publishing house. Today, staying true to this spirit, Collins books are packed with inspiration, innovation and practical expertise. They place you at the centre of a world of possibility and give you exactly what you need to explore it.

Collins. Freedom to teach.

Published by Collins
An imprint of HarperCollins*Publishers*
The News Building
1 London Bridge Street
London
SE1 9GF

HarperCollins*Publishers*
Macken House, 39/40 Mayor Street Upper
Dublin 1, D01 C9W8, Ireland

Browse the complete Collins Caribbean catalogue at
www.collins.co.uk/caribbeanschools

10 9 8 7

ISBN 978-0-00-826330-0

British Library Cataloguing in Publication Data
A catalogue record for this publication is available from the British Library.

Publisher: Elaine Higgleton
Commissioning editor: Tom Hardy
In-house senior editor: Julianna Dunn
Author: Derek McMonagle
Project Manager: Alissa McWhinnie, QBS Learning
Copyeditor: Mitch Fitton
Proofreader: David Hemsley
Photo researcher, illustrator & typesetter: QBS Learning
Cover designer: Gordon MacGilp
Series Designer: Kevin Robbins
Cover photo: Rainer Albiez/Shutterstock
Production controller: Tina Paul
Printed and bound in India by
Replika Press Pvt. Ltd.

This book is produced from independently certified FSC™ paper to ensure responsible forest management . For more information visit: www.harpercollins.co.uk/green

Photo acknowledgments: p22: Carlos Caetano/Shutterstock. p30: pzAxe/Shutterstock, p53: MonikaR/Shutterstock, p70: Taichesco/Shutterstock, p81: Emilio 100/Shutterstock, p87: urbanbuzz/Shutterstock.

The publishers gratefully acknowledge the permission granted to reproduce the copyright material in this book. Every effort has been made to trace copyright holders and to obtain their permission for the use of copyright material. The publishers will gladly receive any information enabling them to rectify any error or omission at the first opportunity.

Contents

1   Science and scientific processes

1.1   Science and scientific processes

1 What is science? _____

_____

                                                   [2]

2 The two areas into which the many branches of science are grouped are natural sciences and _____ sciences.

                                                   [1]

3 Choose which area of study matches each branch of science. Put A, B, C, D, E, F, G, H, I or J in the boxes provided in the right-hand column.

	Branch of science			Area being studied
A	Meteorology			Healing
B	Chemistry			Animals
C	Geology			Living things
D	Medicine			Atmosphere
E	Zoology			Objects beyond Earth
F	Physics			Behaviour of matter
G	Biology			Number, quantity and shape and space
H	Botany			Composition and properties of matter
I	Mathematics			Structures of the Earth
J	Astronomy			Plants

                                                   [5]

4 What is technology? _____

_____

                                                   [2]

5 State three ways in which technology has made your life easier than it would otherwise be.

1 _____

2 _____

3 _____

                                                   [3]

1.2 Impacts of science and technology

1 Describe how the following have been replaced due to science and technology.

a) Horse and cart to carry goods from place to place.

_____

_____

_____

b) Oil lamps to light the home.

_____

_____

_____

c) Larders to keep food from spoiling.

_____

_____

_____

d) Lucky charms to ward off and treat diseases.

_____

_____

_____

[4]

2 Explain the difference between science and technology.

_____

_____

_____

[2]

1.3 Working like a scientist

1 Give the meaning of the following terms.

a) Toxic   _____

b) Flammable   _____

c) Irritant   _____

d) Corrosive   _____

[4]

2 Write the name of the hazard represented by the symbols below using the following words. You may only use each word once.

corrosive   explosive   flammable   harmful   oxidising   toxic

a) _____   b) _____   c) _____

d) _____   e) _____   f) _____

[6]

3 Bleach is toxic, an irritant, corrosive and oxidising. Draw the safety signs you would expect to see on a bottle of bleach.

[4]

1.4 Safety in the school laboratory

1 Explain how each of the following creates a potential hazard in the laboratory and what should be done to avoid the hazard.

a) A student leaves his school bag in the middle of the floor between benches.

_____

_____

_____

_____

b) A student spills dilute hydrochloric acid over the bench at the end of a lesson and doesn't tell her teacher about it.

_____

_____

_____

_____

c) A student eats a sandwich while he carries out a chemical experiment.

_____

_____

_____

_____

d) A student smells an unknown gas by placing the mouth of a test tube immediately below her nose.

_____

_____

_____

_____

[8]

1.5 Famous scientists

Professor Louis Grant was a world famous Jamaican microbiologist. Here are three areas in which he made a significant contribution to the health of people.

In the 1940s, many people in Jamaica suffered from tuberculosis (TB). Professor Grant obtained grants to complete a mass vaccination of children and thus halt the spread of the disease.

In the 1960s, Professor Grant discovered that a disease called leptospirosis was spread through contact with the urine of infected animals, especially rats. He headed a public education campaign to make people aware of the dangers of leaving food exposed and the need to exclude rats from the kitchen.

In the late 1960s, Professor Grant identified that some sick patients had dengue fever. After much research, he concluded that the disease was transmitted by a type of mosquito. This led to a public education campaign that heightened peoples' awareness of the disease and its link to mosquitoes.

1 **a)** Which part of the body is affected by tuberculosis (TB)?

_____

b) What is a vaccination and why is it beneficial?

_____

_____

_____

c) In order to eliminate tuberculosis, why was it necessary to vaccinate all children?

_____

_____

_____

[3]

2 Describe an example in which poor hygiene could lead to a person contracting leptospirosis.

_____

_____

_____

_____

[2]

3 **a)** Name two other diseases spread by mosquitoes.

_____

b) Suggest one thing that people were advised to do to reduce the possibility of being bitten by a disease-carrying mosquito.

_____

_____

[3]

1.6   Scientific skills

1 Describe what each of the following parts of the scientific method involves.

a) Hypothesising: _____

_____

b) Planning: _____

_____

c) Collecting data: _____

_____

d) Recording: _____

_____

e) Reporting: _____

_____

f) Analysing: _____

_____

[6]

2 A scientist proposes that candles burn longer if they are placed in a deep freeze for 24 hours before they are used.

a) What part of the scientific method is this statement? _____

b) Describe how the scientist might investigate this by applying the scientific method.

_____

_____

_____

_____

_____

c) What data will the scientist collect and how will it be recorded?

_____

_____

_____

d) How will the scientist tell if the data supports the hypothesis or not?

_____

_____

_____

[4]

1.7   Carrying out a fair test

1 Zinc reacts with dilute acids to produce hydrogen gas. A student wished to investigate whether different forms of zinc react equally quickly, so he carried out chemical reactions with three different forms of zinc. Details of the reactions are given in the following table.

Form of the zinc	Mass of zinc used / g	Dilute acid used	Volume of acid / cm³	Temperature of acid / °C
One large piece of zinc	2.38	Hydrochloric acid	30	25
Zinc powder	1.56	Hydrochloric acid	30	20
Small pieces of granulated zinc	1.87	Sulfuric acid	25	25

a) i)   What is the variable in this experiment?

_____

ii)   Is this a qualitative or a quantitative variable?

_____

b) Explain why this is not a fair test.

_____

_____

_____

_____

_____

_____

c) Assuming the student alters his method to make a fair test, how would he determine whether the different forms of zinc react equally quickly?

_____

_____

_____

[4]

1.8 Writing a lab report

1 Why is it necessary for scientists to write a detailed report of their experiments?

_____

_____

[2]

2 The following are parts from various lab reports. Identify under which section of the report each should be written.

	Part of lab report	Section of lab report
a)	The flame was green because a reaction had occurred.	
b)	All the rods were of the same thickness.	
c)	The solution was heated over a Bunsen flame.	
d)	It was found that none of the metals could rust.	
e)	To examine the activity of cells under a microscope.	
f)	Acid and alkali reactions.	

[6]

3 Give an example of where each of the following might occur.

a) An experiment needs to be repeated.

_____

_____

_____

b) An experiment follows on from a previous experiment.

_____

_____

_____

[2]

1.9 Engineering design process

1 Here are the seven stages of the engineering design process, but they are not in the correct order. Label the stages A to G according to how they are implemented, starting with A.

_____ build a prototype

_____ carry out suitable research

_____ communicate results

_____ define the problem

_____ generate solutions to the problem

_____ specify the requirements

_____ test and modify the prototype

[7]

2 A company has asked an engineer to design and make a can opener that can be used by people who lack strength in their hands due to conditions like arthritis.

a) Briefly describe how she might carry out research. For example, if she uses the Internet, what key word(s) would she key into the search engine?

_____

_____

_____

_____

b) As a result of her research, the engineer has designed and built two possible devices. Describe how these devices might be tested and the results compared.

_____

_____

_____

_____

c) What will the engineer do as a result of testing?

_____

_____

_____

_____

d) Briefly describe how the engineer might communicate her results to the company.

_____

_____

_____

_____

[4]

1.10 Scientific measurement and SI units

1 Complete the following table with the correct measurement information.

Physical quantity	SI unit	Symbol	One instrument used to measure this quantity
length		m	
	kilogram		balance
time		s	
	kelvin		thermometer

[4]

2 How many metres are in:

a) 1 kilometre? _____ **b)** 1 millimetre? _____

c) 1 centimetre? _____

[3]

3 **a)** How many centimetres are in 1 metre? _____

b) How many square centimetres are in 1 metre^2? _____

c) How many cubic centimetres are in 1 metre^3? _____

d) Give the symbols for the cubic centimetre and the millilitre and state the relationship between them.

_____

[4]

4 Complete the following.

a) 100 °C = _____ K

b) 235 g = _____ kg

c) 50 ml = _____ l

d) 0.35 km = _____ m

e) 4 minutes 18 seconds = _____ s

f) 125 cm³ of water was added to 1.5 dm³ of water. What is the total volume of water in cm³ and in dm³? _____

[6]

1.11 Scientific apparatus

1 Draw the apparatus named in each box below

Conical flask	Test tube	Beaker

[3]

2 Name the apparatus in each box below

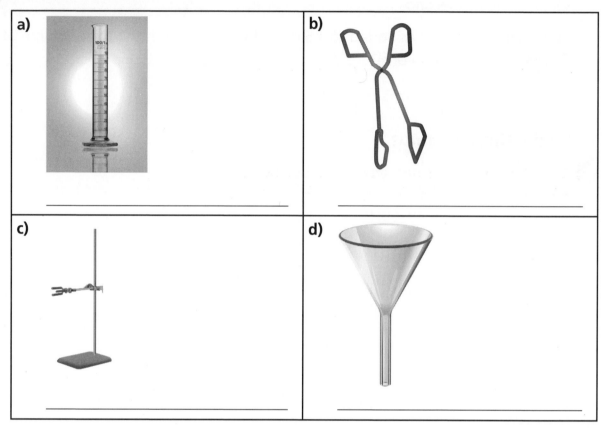

a)

b)

c)

d)

[4]

1.12 Presenting data

1 The following data gives the height of flower seedlings to the nearest centimetre 4 weeks after germination.

16	28	11	17	29	23	9	16	15	16	12	18
8	20	14	9	13	27	19	26	24	7	22	15
21	12	24	23	15	14	20	26	28	19	14	23

a) Complete the following tally chart using the above data.

Height of seedling / cm	Tally	Frequency
6–10		
11–15		
16–20		
21–25		
26–30		
Total		

b) Draw a bar chart on the following grid to present this information.

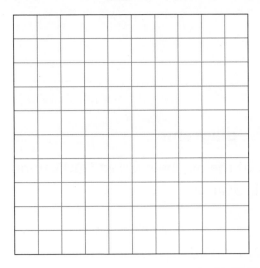

[7]

1.13 Making scientific drawings

1 The following picture shows the apparatus used for the simple distillation of a mixture of acetone and water in the laboratory.

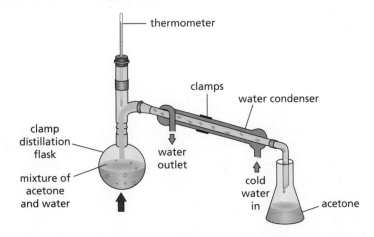

Draw a labelled diagram of the apparatus as it should appear in a lab report.

[8]

1.14 Labelling scientific diagrams

1 Examine the diagram of the eye below. List FOUR things which are incorrect about it for a scientific diagram.

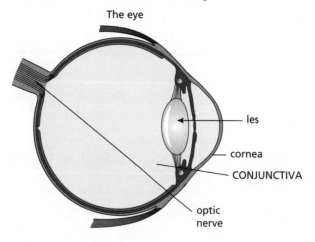

The eye

les

cornea

CONJUNCTIVA

optic
nerve

a) _____

b) _____

c) _____

d) _____

[4]

2 Explain the meaning of the following terms in the context of drawing and labelling diagrams.

a) Annotated _____

_____

b) Magnification _____

_____

c) Specimen _____

_____

d) View _____

_____

[4]

2.1   Nature of matter

1 Classify the pictures on the left under one of the headings on the right based on their state of matter.

[6]

Solids

Liquids

Gases

2.2 Properties of gases

1 State whether each of the following are TRUE or FALSE.

a) All gases have mass. _____

b) All gases are lighter than air. _____

c) All gases have volume. _____

d) All gases support combustion. _____

[4]

2 In an experiment two inflated balloons were hung at either end of a wooden rod which was suspended at the end of a second rod.

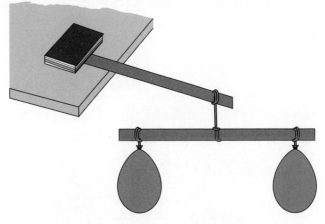

a) What can you say about the masses of gas in the balloons?

_____

b) Explain how you know this.

_____

c) Predict what will happen when one of the balloons is deflated.

_____

d) Explain why this will happen.

_____

[4]

2.3 Density

1 **a)** Explain why the statement 'aluminium is lighter than lead' may be correct or incorrect.

_____

_____

_____

b) Explain why the statement 'aluminium is less dense than lead' is correct.

_____

_____

_____

[2]

2 A hot air balloon has a burner which heats the air inside the balloon envelope.

Explain, in terms of density, why heating the air causes the balloon to float.

_____

_____

_____

[1]

3 **a)** Explain why ice floats on water in terms of density.

_____

_____

b) When 1 cm³ of water freezes is the volume of ice produced less, the same as or more than 1 cm³? Explain your answer.

_____

_____

_____

[2]

2.4 States of matter

1 Describe the position and motion of particles in the following.

a) Solids

_____

_____

_____

b) Liquids

_____

_____

_____

c) Gases

_____

_____

_____

[3]

2 State whether each of the following properties describes a solid, a liquid or a gas. Some properties might describe more than one state.

a) Fixed shape _____

b) Fills the space available _____

c) Can be poured _____

d) Impossible to squash _____

e) Takes the shape of its container _____

[5]

2.5   Particles of matter

1 The particle theory states that _____

_____.

[2]

2 As the amount of energy in matter increases, the bonds between its particles

_____.

[1]

3 State whether each of the following is TRUE or FALSE.

a) When a solid melts its particles slowly cease to exist. _____

b) A solid can stay in one place because its particles are at rest.

_____

c) When you increase the temperature, the speed of particles will increase.

_____

[3]

4 In which states of matter:

a) are particles randomly arranged? _____

b) is there the least attraction between particles? _____

c) are there neatly arranged particles held by strong bonds? _____

[3]

2.6 Properties of solids, liquids and gases

1 In each of the spaces below draw particles to represent each state of matter.

     a) Solid   **b)** Liquid   **c)** Gas

[3]

2 Give two properties of each state of matter.

a) Solids _____

_____

[2]

b) Liquids_____

_____

[2]

c) Gases _____

_____

[2]

3 Both the volume and the shape of matter depend on the _____

_____ between their particles.

[1]

2.7 The effect of heat on matter

1 Explain why the level of liquid in a thermometer rises as the temperature increases.

_____

_____

_____

[1]

2 a) Which of the following substances would melt if heated gently by a small Bunsen flame? Draw a ring around these substances.

aluminium   candle wax   iron   lipstick

b) Is melting a physical change or a chemical change? Explain your answer.

_____

_____

_____

c) How could a liquid be converted back to a solid?

_____

_____

[3]

3 A dish containing butter was left on a sunny windowsill for a few hours.

a) Would the butter change in any way? Explain your answer.

_____

_____

_____

b) If a candle was placed on the same windowsill would it behave in the same way as the butter? Explain your answer.

_____

_____

_____

[2]

4 Describe what happens to the particles of a solid substance that is heated until it melts.

_____

_____

_____

[1]

2.8 Melting and solidifying

1 Melting is the change from _____ to _____.
[2]

2 The temperature of ice is below _____ °C.
[1]

3 As ice melts, its temperature _____.
[1]

4 Dry cobalt chloride paper is blue. In the presence of water it changes to
_____.
[1]

5 As melting occurs, the bonds between the particles of a solid _____.
[1]

6 Solidifying is the change of state from _____ to
_____.
[2]

7 As a liquid solidifies, the bonds between its particles _____.
[1]

8 When matter melts or solidifies, do its chemical properties change? _____
[1]

2.9 Boiling and condensing

1 When a liquid boils it changes to a _____.
[1]

2 Boiling occurs as the temperature of a liquid _____.
[1]

3 The bonds between the particles _____ when a liquid
becomes a gas.
[1]

4 When a substance condenses, its state changes from _____ to
_____.
[2]

5 As condensation occurs, the change in energy of the particles causes them to
come closer and form _____.
[1]

6 To show that water doesn't change after condensation, we use
_____ paper, which turns from blue to pink.
[1]

7 State whether heat is gained or lost:

a) during boiling _____

b) during condensing. _____

[2]

8 **a)** At what temperature does water boil? _____

b) At what temperature does steam condense? _____

[2]

2.10 Evaporation

1 What change of state takes place during evaporation?

_____

[1]

2 The following diagram represents the water cycle.

a) Where does most evaporation take place: at A, B, C or D? _____

b) In what state are the structures at B? _____

c) What is happening at C?

_____

d) What change of state must occur before the process at C can take place?

_____

[4]

3 State two differences between evaporation and boiling.

a) _____

_____

_____

b) _____

_____

_____

[2]

2.11 Sublimation

1 When matter sublimes it changes from _____ to _____.

[2]

2 Since no new substance is formed, sublimation is a _____ process.

[1]

3 Solid _____ _____ is known as dry ice.

[1]

4 Because dry ice sublimes, give one advantage of using it on a stage during a

concert. _____

_____

[1]

5 Desublimation occurs when a substance changes from a _____ to

a _____ .

[2]

6 Decide whether the following statements are TRUE or FALSE.

a) Sublimation is an example of a change of state. _____

b) As substances sublimate, their particles have less energy. _____

c) Whenever water ice gains heat, it undergoes sublimation. _____

d) When solid air fresheners shrink, it is because they undergo sublimation.

_____

[4]

2.12 Heat and expansion

1 Explain each of the following observations.

a) Small gaps are left between lengths of rail on a railway line.

_____

_____

_____

b) Overhead power lines are erected with a small amount of sag.

_____

_____

_____

c) One end of a metal bridge is fixed and the other is set on a giant roller.

_____

_____

_____

[3]

2 Traditionally wagon wheels were made of wooden parts which fitted together without any glue. The wheel was then surrounded by a rim of steel.

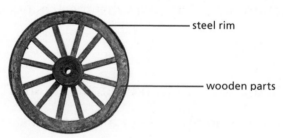

steel rim

wooden parts

Explain why the steel rim was heated until it was red hot, slipped over the wheel and then quickly cooled with water.

_____

_____

_____

_____

[1]

2.13 Diffusion

1 Explain why it is possible to smell fresh-baked bread when walking past a bakery.

_____

_____

_____

[1]

2 The following diagram shows what happened when a small block of a soluble dye was left in a beaker of water overnight.

Explain what happened to the dye.

_____

_____

_____

[1]

3 a) A student placed a sugar cube in a glass of water and left the water to stand. Predict what would happen and explain this in terms of diffusion.

_____

_____

_____

b) Explain, in terms of the rate of diffusion, why people stir their coffee after adding sugar.

_____

_____

c) Is diffusion a physical process or a chemical process? Explain your answer.

_____

_____

[3]

3   Cells and organisms

3.1   Cells and organisms

1 Briefly explain what happens during the following processes.

   a) Photosynthesis _____

   _____

   b) Diffusion _____

   _____

   c) Respiration _____

   _____

                                                                   [3]

2 Which of the characteristics of living things are suggested by the following.

   a) I am three centimetres taller than I was this time last year.

   _____

   b) The plants in the garden produce lots of seeds.

   _____

   c) The dog was able to able to smell where I had hidden its bone.

   _____

   d) Usain Bolt is a very fast runner.

   _____

   e) This morning there were bird droppings all over the car windscreen.

   _____

   f) My favourite meal is rice and peas.

   _____

                                                                    [6]

3 Explain how tissues, organs and cells are related.

   _____

   _____

                                                                    [1]

3.2 Growth

1 Growth is defined as _____

_____.

[1]

2 As some living things grow, such as frogs, they undergo a process called

_____.

[1]

3 Examine this illustration of the growth of a human from a toddler to maturity and answer the questions that follow.

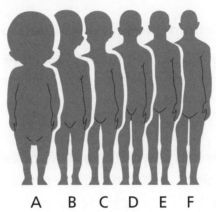

A   B   C   D   E   F

a) Which part of the body grows the most? _____

[1]

b) What fraction of the length of the body of A is the head? _____

[2]

c) What fraction of the length of the body of F is the head? _____

[2]

d) Explain what happens to the proportion of the head to the body as an individual develops from A to F.

_____

_____

[3]

3.3 Respiration

1 The exchange of gases in the lungs is referred to as

_____.

[1]

2 The process by which cells produce energy is described as

_____.

[1]

3 Convert the following information on respiration to a chemical equation.

'In order to obtain energy, glucose and oxygen enter the cell and react, releasing carbon dioxide, which is expelled from the cell.'

_____

[2]

4 In unicellular organisms and plants the uptake of oxygen is carried out by the simple process of diffusion. In mammals, the process of delivering oxygen to the cells requires the help of the internal transport system called the

_____.

[1]

5 The rate of respiration varies. Name ONE way in which the rate can increase.

_____

[1]

3.4 Irritability

1 Irritability means sensitivity and it is the ability of a living thing to

_____.

[1]

2 In the table, name TWO environmental influences that a living thing may be sensitive to and give ONE way it may react to each influence.

	Environmental influence	Reaction
1		
2		

[4]

3 The names of the sense organs are given in the table. Identify ONE stimulus received by each sense organ.

Sense organ	Stimulus
Eyes	
Ears	
Nose	
Tongue	
Skin	

[5]

3.5 Movement

1 Choose whether the following statements are TRUE or FALSE.

a) Movement is the ability to change any position of the body. _____

b) All animals move in the same way. _____

c) Snakes and fish have no legs, so they depend on the strength of their muscles for movement. _____

d) All birds have wings that assist them with movement. _____

e) Of all known animals, centipedes have the most legs. _____

[5]

2 a) Describe how light stimulates plants to move.

_____

_____

b) Explain how the ability to move is an advantage to the plant.

_____

_____

c) State one other stimulus that affects plant growth.

_____

d) Which part of the plant responds to this stimulus?

_____

[4]

3.6   Nutrition

1   Nutrition is concerned with _____

_____.

[1]

2   Green plants produce food using the process of _____.

[1]

3   To obtain nutrients some animals eat plants only and are called _____

_____.

[1]

4   Animals that eat flesh only are called _____.

[1]

5   Why is it necessary for carnivores to have sharp front teeth?

_____.

[2]

6   Crows and vultures are scavengers. Their nutrition consists of _____

_____.

[1]

7   The nutrition of omnivores includes both _____

and _____ material.

[2]

3.7   Excretion

1   Excretion is defined as _____

_____.

[1]

2   What is the name given to the process of the removal of undigested waste
from the gut?

_____

[1]

3 In unicellular organisms and plants excretion is a simple process. In complex mammals, the process requires the help of the _____ _____ which expels waste from the body.

[1]

4 Why is it necessary for organisms to excrete waste products?

_____

_____

[1]

5 State three ways in which plants are able to excrete waste products.

_____

_____

_____

[1]

3.8 Reproduction

1 Reproduction means _____.

[1]

2 There are two types of reproduction, asexual and _____.

[1]

3 Simple organisms with just one cell reproduce by _____ as there is only one parent.

[1]

4 Binary fission and vegetative reproduction are two examples of _____ reproduction.

[1]

5 During sexual reproduction in plants, the male sex cells, called _____ , are transferred to the _____ parts. This process is called _____.

The pollen then combines with female _____ cells, eventually producing seeds.

[4]

6 a) Explain why a banana plant formed from a sucker will be identical to the parent plant.

_____

_____

b) Explain why a child is not identical to either of its parents.

_____

_____

[2]

3.9   What are cells?

1 Cells are defined as _____

_____.

[1]

2 Cells have different shapes because they perform different _____.

[1]

3 Yeast used for making bread is a _____ fungus.

[1]

4 a) An organism contains _____ numbers of cells.

b) A single cell is very _____ and cannot be seen with the unaided eye.

c) Cells are observed using a _____ .

d) This device _____ the cells so that their structure can be seen.

[4]

5 In a human briefly describe the function of:

a) cheek cells _____

b) red blood cells _____

c) nerve cells. _____

[3]

6 In a plant briefly describe the function of:

a) epidermal cells _____

b) leaf cells _____

c) stem cells. _____

[3]

3.10 Using a microscope

1 A microscope must be used to see a cell because _____

_____ .

[1]

2 Name the parts of the microscope indicated by the labelling lines in this diagram.

[7]

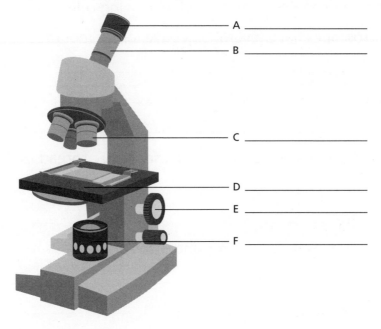

A _____

B _____

C _____

D _____

E _____

F _____

3 On a microscope the eye lens has a magnification of ×5 and the objective lens has a magnification of ×10.

a) What is the overall magnification?

_____

b) What magnification of objective lens would be needed for an overall magnification of ×200?

_____

[2]

3.11 Preparing a specimen of animal cells

1 **a)** Why are specimens of cells sometime stained?

_____

b) What stain is often used on cheek cells?

_____

c) Why might cells be stained with combinations of different dyes?

_____

[3]

2 Explain the following observations when viewing cells.

a) Some microscopes have several objective lenses mounted on a rotating turret.

_____

_____

_____

b) Specimens to be viewed under a microscope are spread as thin as possible.

_____

_____

c) Some microscopes have a mirror under the stage.

_____

_____

_____

[3]

3.12 Structure of an animal cell

1 All the information of a cell is in the DNA of the chromosomes. In what part of the cell are the chromosomes found? _____

[1]

2 State three things found in the cytoplasm of a typical animal cell and explain their function.

1 _____

_____

2 _____

_____

3 _____

_____

[3]

3 Where is the cell membrane found, and what is its function?

_____

_____

_____
[2]

4 Why is the nucleus of a cell sometimes compared to the central processor of a computer?

_____

_____

_____
[1]

3.13 Preparing a specimen of plant cells

1 **a)** Where in an onion can a thin layer of epidermal cells be found?

_____

b) How many cells thick is this layer?

_____

c) Describe how a sample of this layer can be obtained.

_____

_____

_____
[3]

2 **a)** What stain is usually used on the epidermal cells of an onion?

_____

b) What colour are the cells after staining?

_____

c) Briefly describe the shape of the cells.

_____
[3]

3 **a)** What is wicking?

_____

_____

b) Describe when and how wicking is carried out during the preparation of a specimen of onion cells.

_____

_____

_____

_____

[2]

3.14   Structure of plant cells

1 The following model shows some features of a typical plant cell.

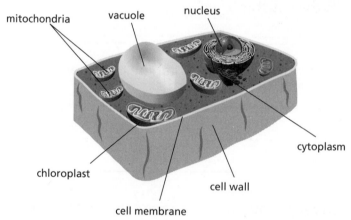

Which of the parts labelled in the diagram:

a) contains the green pigment chlorophyll? _____

b) controls the processes in the cell? _____

c) gives the cell a rigid structure? _____

d) provides the cell with energy? _____

e) contains starch grains? _____

f) controls movement of substances into and out of the cell? _____

[6]

2 a) Name a structure that would be found in a leaf cell but not a root cell.

_____

b) Explain why this structure is not found in a root cell.

_____

_____

[2]

3 a) Name three structures that would be found both in a typical animal cell and a typical plant cell.

_____

_____

b) What structure in an animal cell serves the same function as starch grains in a plant cell?

_____

c) Name two other structures that would be found in a typical plant cell that would be absent from a typical animal cell.

_____

[3]

3.15 Cells, tissues and organs

1 Name the organs of the digestive system.

_____

_____

[3]

2 Name three systems in the human body other than the digestive system.

a) _____

b) _____

c) _____

[3]

3 **a)** Identify the organs labelled A to E in the diagram of a flowering plant.

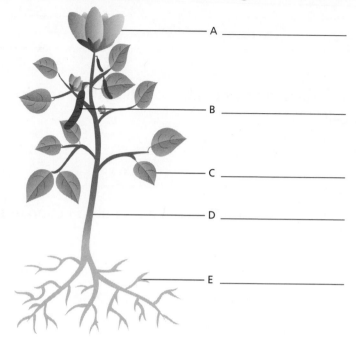

A _____

B _____

C _____

D _____

E _____

[5]

b) Briefly describe the role of the following organs.

A _____

C _____

E _____

[3]

3.16 Unicellular organisms

1 What does unicellular mean?

_____

[1]

2 Name the following unicellular organism.

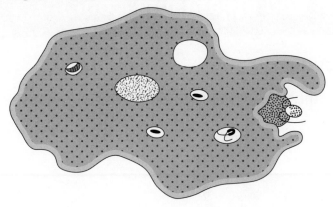

_____

[1]

3 Briefly explain how the unicellular organism in the previous question exhibits the following characteristics of all living organisms.

a) Nutrition _____

_____

b) Reproduction _____

_____

c) Respiration _____

_____

d) Movement _____

_____

e) Irritability _____

_____

[5]

3.17 Respiratory system

1 Add the labels to this diagram to name the parts of the respiratory system.

[4]

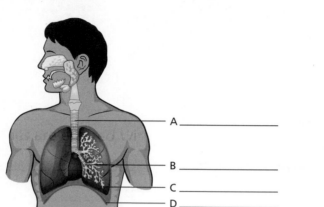

A _____

B _____

C _____

D _____

2 In which part of the lungs are oxygen and carbon dioxide exchanged?

_____

[1]

3 When you inhale, the volume of the lungs _____.

[1]

3.18 Circulatory system

1 What is the circulatory system responsible for?_____

_____

_____

[2]

2 Why is it necessary for the arteries to be thick and muscular? _____

_____

[2]

3 a) What pushes blood along veins?

_____

b) Why do long veins have valves?

_____

[2]

4 **a)** What information does pulse rate give?

_____

b) Where on the arm is pulse rate often taken?

_____

c) In what range is the pulse rate of an average adult?

_____

[3]

5 For each of the following state whether the blood is oxygenated (O) or deoxygenated (D).

a) Blood travelling from the lungs to the heart _____

b) Blood travelling from the rest of the body to the heart _____

c) Blood travelling from the heart to the rest of the body _____

d) Blood travelling from the heart to the lungs _____

[4]

3.19 Digestive system

1 What is the purpose of the digestive system? _____

_____

[1]

2 The first place digestion occurs in the body is the _____ .

[1]

Use this diagram to answer questions 3–6.

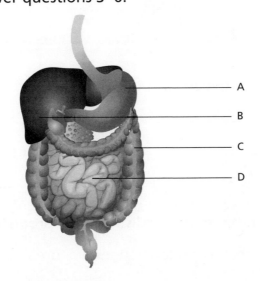

3 Which system is represented by this diagram?

a) Nervous   b) Digestive   c) Alimentary canal

[1]

4 On the diagram, A represents:

a) one lung   b) a kidney   c) the stomach.

[1]

5 The function of C is to:

a) absorb water   b) add chemicals to faeces   c) keep the gut contained.

[1]

6 What happens in D?

a) Digestion is completed.   b) Toxins are neutralised.

c) Alcohol absorption occurs.

[1]

3.20 Excretory system

1 Name the parts of the excretory system by adding the missing labels.

A _____

B _____

C _____

[3]

2 Explain the difference between excretion and egestion.

_____

_____

_____

[1]

3 Circle the substances in the following list that are products of excretion.

sweat   vomit   carbon dioxide   urine   urea   faeces

[5]

4 Explain the role of the skin as an excretory organ.

_____

_____

_____

[1]

5 Explain why exhaled air contains a much higher concentration of carbon dioxide than inhaled air.

_____

_____

_____

[1]

3.21 Skeletal and muscular systems

1 Name two parts of the skeletal system that provide protection for body organs and state which organs they protect.

_____

_____

_____

[2]

2 What do the skeletal system and muscular system together allow the body to do?

_____

[1]

3 **a)** Which is the longest bone in the human skeleton?

_____

b) How many bones are between the elbow and the wrist?

_____

c) Name a place on the body where there is a ball and socket joint.

_____

d) Compare the movement of a hinge joint with the movement of a ball and socket joint.

_____

_____

_____

[4]

3.22 Reproductive system

1 What is the function of the reproductive system? _____

_____

[1]

2 Some parts of the male and female reproductive systems in these diagrams are identified by letters. Write the letter next to the correct name given in the tables that follow.

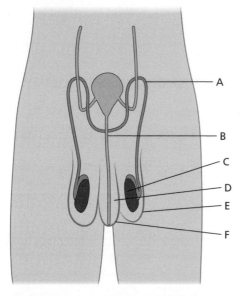

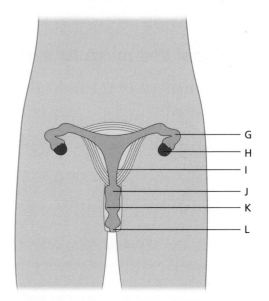

Male reproductive system

Part	Letter
penis	
sperm duct	
testis	
urethra	
foreskin	
scrotum	

Female reproductive system

Part	Letter
oviduct	
ovary	
uterine lining	
vagina	
cervix	
opening of vagina	

[6]

3.23 Specialised animal cells

1 What is a specialised cell?

_____.

[1]

2 Below are some specialised cells. In the second column write the function of each type of cell.

[3]

	Specialised cell	Function
a)		
b)		
c)		
d)		
e)		
f)		

3.24 Plant systems

1 State two functions of each of the following parts of a plant.

a) Roots _____

_____

b) Leaves _____

_____

c) Stem _____

_____

[6]

2 Explain the following observations as fully as you can.

a) Roots generally divide many times in the soil.

_____

_____

_____

b) Leaves are usually large and flat.

_____

_____

_____

c) Flowers are often highly coloured and scented.

_____

_____

_____

[3]

3.25 Specialised plant cells

1 **a)** Identify the specialist plant cells shown at the centre of the following diagram.

_____

b) On which part of a plant are these mostly found?

_____

c) What is the function of these cells?

_____

d) Explain how these cells carry out this function.

_____

_____

_____

[4]

2 **a)** Draw a labelled diagram of a root hair cell.

[4]

b) Explain how the shape of the cell is suited to its function.

_____

_____

_____

[2]

4 Energy

4.1 Energy

1 The term used for stored energy is _____. [1]

2 Moving energy is referred to as _____. [1]

3 Which sense organ of the body can detect the following forms of energy?

a) Light energy _____

b) Heat energy _____

c) Sound energy _____ [3]

4 Name something that is associated with each of the following forms of energy.

a) Chemical energy and electrical energy

_____

b) Heat energy and light energy

_____

c) Nuclear energy and electricity

_____

d) Potential energy and kinetic energy

_____ [4]

4.2 Potential energy

1 For each diagram, choose whether it shows the gravitational, chemical or elastic form of potential energy.

a) A man close to the edge of a ledge. 	b) A slingshot ready to be released. 
_____	_____

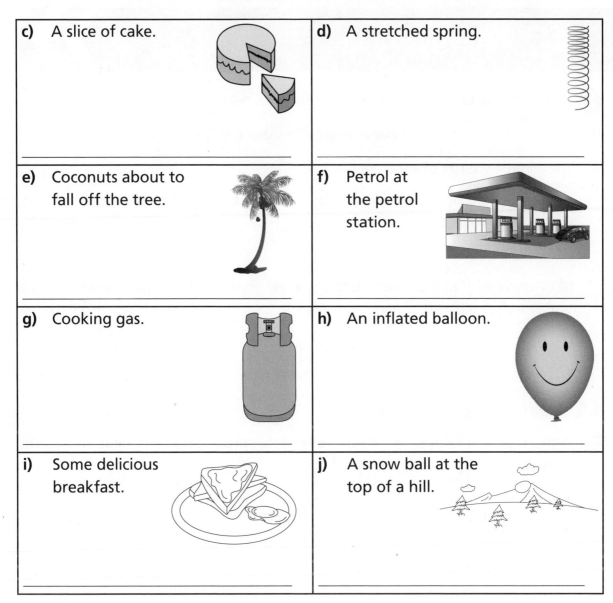

c) A slice of cake.		**d)** A stretched spring.	
e) Coconuts about to fall off the tree.		**f)** Petrol at the petrol station.	
g) Cooking gas.		**h)** An inflated balloon.	
i) Some delicious breakfast.		**j)** A snow ball at the top of a hill.	

[10]

4.3 Kinetic energy

The amount of kinetic energy depends on an object's mass and speed.

1 For each statement, circle the one which has the greater kinetic energy from each pair.

a)	Rolling at the same speed.	**b)**	Falling from the same height.
	A marble		A chair
	A basket ball		A boulder
c)	Pitching two identical balls.	**d)**	Travelling in a car.
	Ball 1 by a test match cricketer		At 30 km per hour
	Ball 2 by a 6-year-old child		At 60 km per hour

[4]

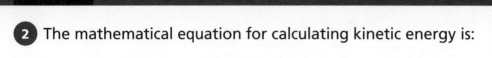

2 The mathematical equation for calculating kinetic energy is:

$$\text{kinetic energy} = \tfrac{1}{2}\ \text{mass} \times \text{velocity}^2$$

The kinetic energy of an object is x.

a) What would be the kinetic energy of an object with twice the mass moving at the same velocity?

_____

b) What would be the kinetic energy of an object of the same mass moving at twice the velocity?

_____

[2]

4.4   Heat and light energy

1 The _____ is a source of energy, producing both heat and light energy for use on Earth.

[1]

2 a) Explain why an object may cast a shadow.

_____

_____

_____

b) Complete the diagram by showing the shadow cast by the ball on the screen.

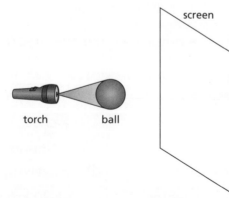

c) Predict what would happen to the size of the shadow formed by the ball if the screen was moved further away from it.

_____

[3]

4.5 Sound energy

For questions 1–3, circle the correct answer.

1 Why is there no sound in space?

a) It is too far for sound to travel.

b) Sound waves are absorbed.

c) There is no matter to carry sound.

d) Sound vibrations are too small.

2 What does sound travel the fastest through?

a) Solid   b) Liquid   c) Gel   d) Gas

3 What are sound waves that are regular and organised, making them pleasing to the ear, called?

a) Music   b) Drum beats   c) Cacophony   d) Noise

[3]

4 Fill in the blanks with the correct word to complete this paragraph.

Sound occurs when objects _____. Vibrating objects pass sounds

to our _____ so we can hear. Sound is able to _____

through matter. In a _____ there is no matter to transmit sound.

The more _____ there are in the vibrations, the louder the sound is.

[5]

4.6   Electrical energy

1 This table gives the amount of electrical energy used by a family for each appliance for one hour. The electric company charges 70¢ per kWh. Study the table and answer the questions that follow to find the cost of their electricity bill for one day.

Electrical appliance	Consumption (kW) per hour
Air conditioning	3.5
Water heater	2.2
100 W bulbs	0.1
Computer	0.8
Iron	1.4
Refrigerator	0.6

Cost

a) Air conditioner for 6 hours   = 6 × 3.5 × 70¢   = _____

b) Water heater for 3 hours   = 3 × 2.2 × 70¢   = _____

c) 6 light bulbs, each for 4 hours   =   = _____

d) Computer for 8 hours   =   = _____

e) Iron for 1½ hours   =   = _____

f) Refrigerator 24 hours   =   = _____

     Total cost for one day   = _____

g) The number of kWh of electricity usage is adjusted for ALL customers. If that adjustment were not made, what would be the electricity bill for only these appliances for this family for a 30-day month?

_____ × 30

= _____

[8]

4.7 Nuclear energy

1 Decide whether the following statements are TRUE or FALSE.

a) Nuclear energy is produced in power plants as a result of nuclear fission.

_____

b) When uranium atoms are split, thermal energy is released. _____

c) A disadvantage of splitting uranium is that too little energy is produced.

_____

d) Animals but not plants are affected by nuclear energy pollution. _____

[4]

2 Identify the disadvantage of using nuclear energy.

a) Radioactive wastes are produced.

b) Air pollution occurs.

c) Fission produces small amounts of energy.

d) Fusion produces too much energy.

[2]

3 In fusion small atoms combine to form larger ones, but in nuclear fission

_____

_____ .

[1]

4.8 Non-renewable energy sources

1 From the sources of energy shown here, circle the non-renewable ones.

Natural Gas — Comfortable. Responsible. Geothermal HYDROPOWER SOLAR ENERGY

Biomass energy

[5]

2 Give TWO disadvantages of fossil fuels.

a) _____

b) _____

[2]

For questions 3–4, circle the correct answer.

3 A non-renewable resource is one that is:

a) non-replaceable

b) replaced slower than it is used

c) found deep in the Earth's crust

d) not possible to exhaust.

4 Which of these energy sources is non-renewable?

a) Solar   **b)** Wind   **c)** Natural gas   **d)** Biomass

[3]

4.9   Renewable energy sources

For questions 1–2, circle the correct answer.

1 Some sources of energy are renewable because they:

a) can be naturally replenished within a short period of time

b) are all clean and free to use

c) can change easily from one form to another

d) are not factors of pollution.

[1]

2 Which of these is a renewable resource of energy?

a) Geothermal   **b)** Solar   **c)** Wind   **d)** All of these

[1]

3 Choose the answer which matches each of the following. Put the correct letter into the box provided in the table.

A Sun   B Wind turbine   C Biofuel

D Hydroelectricity   E Geothermal   F Solar panel

	Original source of renewable energy
	Often associated with dams
	Only works when the wind blows
	Uses light from the Sun
	Can be made from plant material
	Energy from hot rocks

4.10 Biofuels

1 Whereas many forms of energy are made from non-living matter, biofuels are

made from _____ materials.

[1]

2 The primary energy source for animals and plants is:

a) water   **b)** fertiliser   **c)** sunlight   **d)** nutrients in the soil.

[1]

3 Choose TRUE or FALSE for each of these statements.

a) Biofuel is fuel from non-fossilised organic matter. _____

b) Both petroleum and biofuels are from the same source. _____

c) The energy stored by plants is used as biofuel. _____

d) Many plants contain oil in their seeds. _____

e) Sunflower oil from the grocery store cannot be used as biofuel. _____

[5]

4 **a)** What is the main component of the fuel gas made by digesting animal dung?

_____

b) What happens to the residue that remains when the fuel gas has been removed?

_____

c) The fuel gas contains carbon dioxide. How can this be removed?

_____

[3]

4.11 Transforming energy

1 Use linking lines to match each object with the correct energy outputs.

a)

| Light |
| Heat |
| Sound |
| Movement |

b)

| Sound |
| Light |
| Movement |
| Heat |

c)

| Light |
| Heat |
| Sound |
| Movement |

d)

| Sound |
| Light |
| Movement |
| Heat |

e)

| Light |
| Heat |
| Sound |
| Movement |

f)

| Sound |
| Light |
| Movement |
| Heat |

[6]

4.12 Sankey diagrams

1 An energy-saving bulb is shown here.

Of the energy that an energy-saving bulb produces, only 60% is transferred as light; the rest is converted to heat.

a) What percentage is wasted as heat? _____

[1]

A representation of the energy produced by the bulb has been started on the graph below. Each 2 mm represents 10%.

b) Complete the Sankey diagram to show how the energy is distributed.

[2]

c) Identify each separation of the Sankey diagram.

[2]

4.13 Conservation of energy (1)

1 Why is it necessary for governments to seek renewable sources of energy?

_____

_____

[1]

2 a) In what year did the Jamaican Government adopt a National Energy Policy relating to making more use of renewable energy sources? _____

b) What is the target in terms of percentage of the country's needs from renewable energy sources by 2030? _____

c) What percentage of the country's needs is currently met by renewable energy sources? _____

[3]

3 Although renewable energy sources have many advantages they also have their limitations. State one limitation or disadvantage associated with the following.

a) A wind turbine _____

_____

b) A solar panel _____

_____

c) A tidal barrage _____

_____

[3]

4.14 Conservation of energy (2)

1 Everyone can do a little to conserve energy. Below is a crossword puzzle. Use the clues on conserving energy to complete the puzzle.

Across

1. _____ full loads in machine

4. _____ using 150 watt bulbs

8. _____ a garden

11. _____ paper and plastic

13. _____ tap while brushing your teeth

15. _____ a bike instead of driving

16. _____ curtains when it is hot

17. _____ on both sides of paper

18. _____ to energy saving bulbs

Down

1. _____ warm clothes when it is cold

2. _____ clothes outside to dry

3. _____ smaller cars

5. _____ outdoors instead of watch TV for recreation

6. _____ appliances when on vacation

7. _____ kettle on gas

9. Close a _____ tap

10. _____ showers instead of baths

12. _____ off TV when no one is watching

14. _____ off lights in an empty room

[10]

4.15 Energy and the Caribbean countries

1 **a)** What problem do all Caribbean countries share with regard to large-scale sources of energy?

_____

_____

b) Why is this a problem?

_____

c) What general strategy are all countries adopting in different ways?

_____

_____

[3]

2 In which part of Trinidad and Tobago is there a plan to build a wind farm? Explain why this location was chosen.

_____

_____

_____

[2]

3 **a)** Where in the Caribbean has a geothermal power station been producing electricity for over 30 years?

_____

b) Explain how a geothermal power station produces electricity.

_____

_____

_____

[2]

c) Would a geothermal power station be an option for any country in the Caribbean? Explain your answer.

_____

_____

_____

[2]

5.1   Plant reproduction

1   **a)** Complete the following diagram by naming the different stages in the life cycle of a flowering plant.

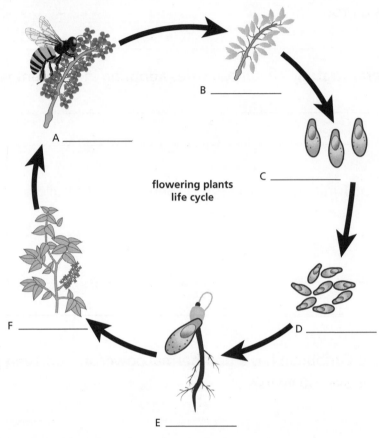

B _____

A _____

flowering plants
life cycle

C _____

F _____

D _____

E _____

[6]

b) Which of these processes involve something being removed from the plant? State what is removed by each process.

_____

_____

_____

[3]

5.2 Flower structure

1 The diagram shows the parts A to H of a flower.

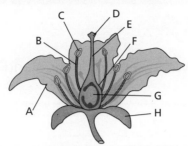

a) In which part is pollen produced? _____

b) Which part attracts insects? _____

c) Which part is an anther? _____

d) Which part is the style? _____

e) Which part will develop into a seed? _____

f) Which parts make up the pistil?

_____

g) What collective name is given to parts B and C?

_____

h) Describe the role of part H.

_____

_____

i) Name one other part of a flower which is not labelled in the above diagram and describe its function.

_____

_____

_____

[10]

5.3   Pollination

1 Explain the difference between self-pollination and cross pollination.

_____

_____

_____

[2]

2 The following diagram shows details of a flower.

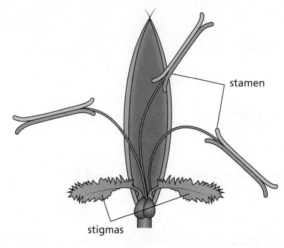

State and explain three pieces of evidence from the diagram which indicate that this plant is pollinated by wind.

1 _____

_____

_____

2 _____

_____

_____

3 _____

_____

_____

[3]

5.4 Fertilisation and seed formation

1 Label the parts in the diagram which show a stage during fertilisation.

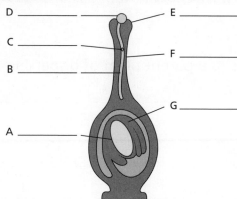

D _____ _____
C _____ _____
B _____ _____
E _____
F _____
G _____
A _____ _____

[7]

2 **a)** Explain how a male gamete is able to fuse with a female gamete after pollination has taken place.

_____

_____

_____

_____

b) Which part(s) on the diagram will eventually become a seed?

_____

c) Which part(s) on the diagram will eventually become a fruit?

_____

[3]

3 **a)** Give two examples of succulent fruits.

_____

b) Give two examples of non-succulent fruits.

_____

[4]

5.5   Dispersal

1   Explain two advantages to a parent plant of dispersing its seeds.

1 _____

_____

_____

2 _____

_____

_____

[2]

2   The following photograph shows fruits from a dandelion flower.

Describe three ways in which these fruits are suited to wind dispersal.

1 _____

_____

_____

2 _____

_____

_____

3 _____

_____

_____

[3]

5.6 Germination

1 The following diagram shows the structure of a seed.

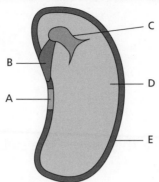

a) What will structure B develop into?

_____

b) What will structure C develop into?

_____

c) Name and state the functions of the following parts of the seed.

   i) Part A _____

     _____

  ii) Part D _____

     _____

 iii) Part E _____

     _____

[5]

5.7 Asexual reproduction in plants

1 **a)** How is asexual reproduction different from sexual reproduction?

_____

_____

_____

b) Why is asexual reproduction sometimes called vegetative reproduction?

_____

_____

c) What is a clone?

_____

_____

[3]

2 Some plants, like irises, form a rhizome in the soil. This provides a means for the plant to reproduce asexually.

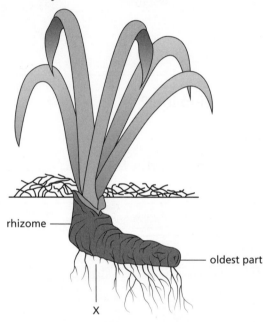

a) What happens to the length of the rhizome each year?

_____

b) Predict what would happen if the rhizome was cut at point X.

_____

_____

c) Will all the irises obtained from a single rhizome be the same or different? Explain your answer.

_____

_____

_____

[3]

5.8 Commercial importance of vegetative reproduction

1 The following sequence of diagrams shows a process called bud grafting.

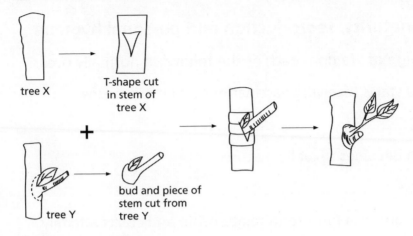

tree X

T-shape cut
in stem of
tree X

+

tree Y

bud and piece of
stem cut from
tree Y

a) Describe the stages of bud grafting.

_____

_____

_____

_____

_____

b) Predict what would happen if the graft didn't take.

_____

_____

c) How could this process create a tree that produced two varieties of apple?

_____

_____

_____

[3]

6 Sexual maturity, reproduction and personal hygiene

6.1 Sexual maturity, reproduction and personal hygiene

1 At what stage of life does each of the following normally occur?

a) A person starts receiving vaccinations against diseases.

_____

b) A person becomes sexually mature.

_____

c) A person enters a long-term relationship and starts a family.

_____

d) A person starts their schooling.

_____

[4]

2 Here are some actions you carry out as part of your personal hygiene and care. State whether you would normally carry these out:

several times each day   once each day   once every several days

a) Clean your teeth   _____

b) Change your underwear _____

c) Wash your hands   _____

d) Take a shower   _____

e) Trim your nails   _____

f) Comb your hair   _____

g) Polish your shoes   _____

[7]

6.2 Infancy and childhood

1 a) Why are babies vaccinated against diseases?

_____

_____

b) Name two diseases for which vaccination is usually given.

_____

_____

c) How is a vaccination usually given to a baby?

_____

_____

[4]

2 **a)** What is nourishment?

_____

_____

b) State and explain two ways in which poor nourishment might affect the development of a child.

_____

_____

_____

_____

c) Explain how a child might have lots of food to eat yet they may still be malnourished.

_____

_____

_____

[4]

6.3 Adolescence and adulthood

1 Adolescence is often considered a difficult and sometimes emotional time. Suggest three aspects of adolescent behaviour which might reflect this.

a) _____

_____

_____

b) _____

_____

_____

c) _____

_____

_____

[3]

2 a) Explain the difference between adolescence and puberty.

_____

_____

_____

b) Do boys and girls enter puberty at the same age? Explain your answer.

_____

_____

_____

[2]

6.4 How are we different?

1 The following table shows the number of students in different height ranges in a class.

Height in cm	Number of students
140–144	2
145–149	3
150–154	6
155–159	8
160–164	9
165–169	4
170–174	2
175–179	1
Total	

a) Complete the table by giving the total number of students in the class.

[1]

b) Draw a bar chart to represent this information.

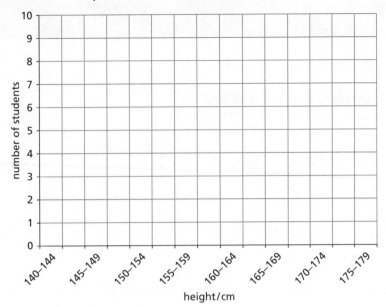

[1]

c) i) What height range contains the most students?

_____

ii) How many students are in this range? _____

[2]

6.5 The male reproductive system

1 The following diagram shows details of the male reproductive system.

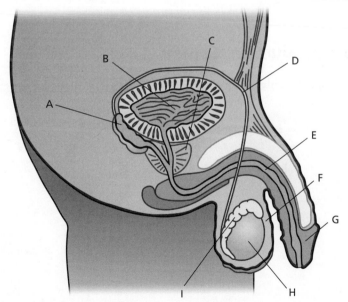

a) Which part is the sperm duct? _____

b) Give an alternative name for the sperm duct. _____

c) In which part are sperm formed? _____

d) What are the names of parts A and C?

   A = _____   C = _____

e) What are the functions of parts A and C?

_____

_____

f) What is stored in part B? _____

g) Where does the substance stored in part B come from?

_____

_____

h) Name part H.   _____

i) What advantage is there in having part H outside the main body cavity?

_____

_____

[11]

6.6 The female reproductive system

1 The diagram shows details of the female reproductive system.

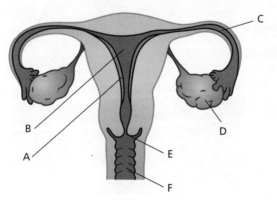

a) Which part is the oviduct? _____

b) By what other name is the oviduct known? _____

c) In which part are egg cells produced? _____

d) Which part is also known as the womb? _____

e) In which part will the placenta develop during pregnancy? _____

f) What is part E and what is its function?

_____

_____

[6]

6.7   The menstrual cycle

1 At what age does a female typically:

a) start to have regular menstrual cycles? _____

b) stop having regular menstrual cycles? _____

[2]

2 Describe the role of each of the following hormones in the menstrual cycle as fully as you can.

a) Follicle stimulating hormone (FSH) _____

_____

_____

b) Oestrogen_____

_____

_____

c) Luteinising hormone (LH) _____

_____

_____

d) Progesterone _____

_____

_____

[4]

6.8 Sexual reproduction

1 **a)** Give the names of the two sex cells involved in fertilisation in humans.

_____

b) What do the cells form after fertilisation?

_____

c) Where does fertilisation normally take place?

_____

d) How long after fertilisation is a ball of cells formed?

_____

[4]

2 **a)** Explain how the female body prepares for the development of an embryo.

_____

_____

_____

b) Describe the role of oestrogen and progesterone in this process.

_____

_____

_____

[2]

6.9 Personal hygiene

1 Explain each of the following as fully as you can.

a) When washing, a person pays particular attention to their arm pits.

_____

_____

_____

b) It is not sensible to clean wax from the ears with the point of a pencil.

_____

_____

_____

c) In addition to brushing their teeth, people may also use dental floss or an interdental brush.

_____

_____

_____

[3]

2 A personal hygiene product is shown in the photograph.

a) What two functions does the product serve according to the label?

_____

[2]

b) Describe the action of each of these functions.

_____

_____

_____

[2]

7 Sexually transmitted infections and drugs

7.1 Sexually transmitted infections and drugs

1 **a)** What is an STI?

_____

b) How does a person catch an STI?

_____

_____

[2]

2 State whether each of the following is TRUE or FALSE.

a) Condoms prevent the transfer of STIs if used correctly. _____

b) All STIs only cause the body mild discomfort. _____

c) STIs are examples of communicable infections. _____

d) STIs don't need to be treated and will clear up themselves over time. _____

e) Condoms are available for men and for women. _____

[5]

3 **a)** What is a drug?

_____

_____

b) Name a drug that you might take for a headache. _____

c) Name a drug that you might take for stomach ache. _____

d) Why might a person take a drug when they are not ill?

_____

_____

[4]

7.2 Herpes, chlamydia and human papilloma virus (HPV)

1 **a)** What organism causes herpes?

_____

b) What are the visible symptoms of herpes?

_____

c) What is the treatment for herpes and does this rid the body of the microorganism which causes it?

_____

_____

_____

[4]

2 **a)** What type of microorganism causes chlamydia?

_____

b) Why might a person be unaware that they have chlamydia?

_____

_____

c) Does this mean that they cannot pass the microorganism on to others?

_____

d) What type of drug is used to treat chlamydia?

_____

[4]

3 **a)** What does HPV stand for?

_____

b) Which part of the body is affected by HPV?

_____

c) How can the condition be cured? Explain your answer.

_____

_____

_____

[3]

7.3 Gonorrhoea, syphilis and HIV

1 **a)** By what common name is gonorrhoea known?

_____

b) Describe the symptoms of gonorrhoea.

_____

_____

_____

c) What type of drug is used to treat gonorrhoea?

_____

[3]

2 **a)** What do the following letters stand for?

   i) HIV _____

   ii) AIDS _____

b) Describe the link between HIV and AIDS.

_____

_____

_____

_____

[3]

7.4 Interpreting data on STIs

1 The following graph shows the reported cases of the herpes simplex virus (HSV) in Jamaica between 1959 and 2003.

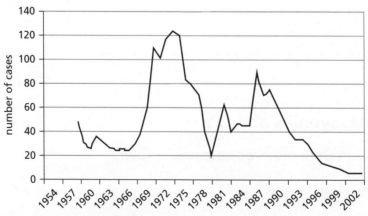

(Source: West Indian Medical Journal)

a) Estimate the period when the number of cases was 100 or more per year.

_____

b) Estimate the period when the number of cases was 20 or less per year.

_____

c) What is the general trend of cases of HSV from 1990 to 2003?

_____

d) Suggest a reason why there was a peak in the number of cases around 1975.

_____

_____

e) Predict how the pattern of number of cases would continue after 2003 if people who contracted HSV:

   i)   obtained medical treatment as soon as possible

     _____

   ii) didn't bother to get treatment for several weeks.

     _____

[6]

7.5 Transmission and prevention of STIs

1 **a)** Where should a person go to obtain advice about STIs?

_____

b) Where should a person go if they suspect they have an STI?

_____

c) What is meant by a 'walk-in service'?

_____

_____

d) Suggest circumstances in which a person would find it useful to have a walk-in service.

_____

_____

_____

[4]

2 The following graphs show the AIDS cases per 100 000 population between 1982 and 2007 for Kingston/St Andrew, for St James and for Jamaica as a whole.

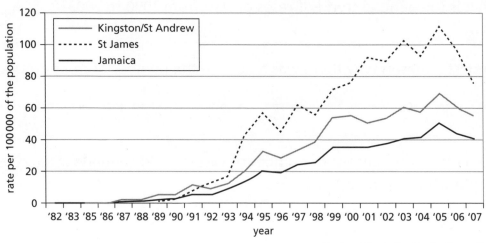

(Source: West Indian Medical Journal)

a) During what period did cases start to rapidly increase? _____

b) Is the prevalence of AIDS in St James typical of Jamaica as a whole? Explain your answer.

_____

_____

_____

c) The prevalence of AIDS in Kingston/St Andrew in 2007 was 55.3 per 100 000 population. If the population was 600 000 how many cases of AIDS were there?

_____

_____

_____

[4]

7.6 Drug use

1 The photograph shows the front of a packet of the drug Panadol.

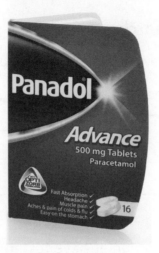

a) What type of drug is Panadol in terms of its availability?

_____

b) Name two conditions for which a person might take Panadol.

_____

_____

c) What mass of paracetamol is contained in a single tablet of Panadol? Give this in grams.

_____

[3]

2 a) What is needed to obtain a pharmacy drug?

_____

b) Suggest a reason why the availability of a drug might be restricted.

_____

_____

_____

[2]

7.7 The ethics of drug research

1 Describe two reasons why new drugs are always being made.

1 _____

_____

2 _____

_____

[2]

2 In the past some cosmetic companies have tested new shampoos by introducing them to the eyes of animals like rabbits to find out if they cause irritation.

a) Explain why a person might agree to the use of animal testing of a new drug, such as a painkiller, but object to the use of animals to test cosmetic products.

_____

_____

_____

_____

_____

_____

b) Suggest an alternative way in which cosmetic products could be tested.

_____

_____

_____

_____

[2]

7.8 Drug abuse

1 **a)** Explain the difference between drug use and drug abuse.

_____

_____

_____

_____

b) Suggest three reasons why drug abuse is harmful to the individual.

1 _____

_____

2 _____

_____

3 _____

_____

c) What is a drug overdose and why is it potentially dangerous?

_____

_____

_____

_____

[5]

2 Why are recreational drugs like cocaine and heroin often associated with crime?

_____

_____

_____

_____

_____

[1]

8.1   Climate change

1   Describe three ways in which decisions made by Government can reduce damage to the environment.

1 _____

_____

2 _____

_____

3 _____

_____

[3]

2   Describe three ways in which decisions made by an individual can reduce damage to the environment.

1 _____

_____

2 _____

_____

3 _____

_____

[3]

3   Explain the links between the greenhouse effect, global warming and climate change.

_____

_____

_____

_____

_____

_____

[2]

8.2 Global warming

1 The following diagram shows the boundary of sea ice surrounding the North Pole in 1979 and today.

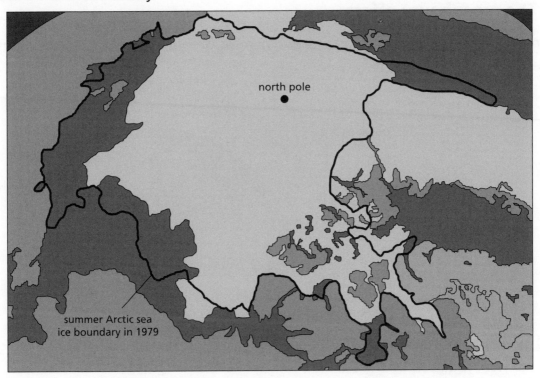

summer Arctic sea
ice boundary in 1979

a) What has happened to the sea ice boundary over this period?

_____

b) Suggest a reason for this change.

_____

_____

c) Describe the effect of this change on the average sea level.

_____

_____

d) Suggest what effect this will have on the coastline of a country.

_____

_____

[4]

8.3 The greenhouse effect

1 The following diagram represents the layer of greenhouse gases surrounding the Earth.

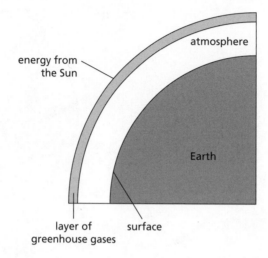

a) Complete the diagram by showing the effect of the layer of greenhouse gases on heat radiated by the Earth.

b) Briefly describe the effects of the layer of greenhouse gases.

_____

_____

_____

c) The layer of greenhouse gases has existed for many millions of years. Explain why, as far as scientists are aware, it has only become a problem over the last 200 years.

_____

_____

_____

_____

[3]

8.4 Greenhouse gases

1 **a)** Give the names of three gases, other than carbon dioxide, that make a significant contribution to the greenhouse effect.

_____

b)

i) Draw a line on the grid to show how the concentration of carbon dioxide has changed from 1800 to the present day.

ii) Extend your line by adding a broken line to show how the concentration of atmospheric carbon dioxide will change between now and 2050 if nothing is done to reduce emissions of this gas.

[3]

2 The greenhouse index of CFCs is 23 000 while the index of carbon dioxide is 1.

a) What is the greenhouse index of a gas?

_____

_____

b) Explain why the contribution made by carbon dioxide to the greenhouse effect is far greater than that made by CFCs even though the greenhouse index of CFCs is much greater.

_____

_____

_____

[2]

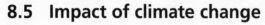
8.5   Impact of climate change

1 The following graph shows how the average sea level at a location changed over the 20th century from a base line in 1900.

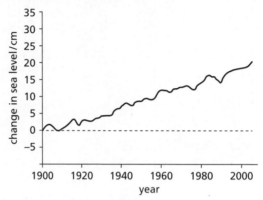

a) i)   What trend is shown by the graph?

_____

   ii)   Suggest why the graph is not a straight line.

_____

_____

b) Explain the trend shown by the graph.

_____

_____

_____

_____

[3]

c) The Maldives is a country in the Indian Ocean consisting of many small islands. The average height of the land is 120 cm above sea level.

Why is the population of the Maldives particularly worried by changes in the sea level?

_____

_____

_____

_____

[1]

8.6 Reducing climate change

1 a) What is a carbon dioxide sink?

_____

_____

_____

b) Explain how each of the following acts as a natural carbon dioxide sink.

i) A forest _____

_____

_____

ii) An ocean _____

_____

_____

[3]

2 Explain how each of the following Government policies will reduce atmospheric carbon dioxide levels.

a) Making greater use of renewable energy sources.

_____

_____

_____

_____

b) Replacing petrol and diesel powered cars with electrically driven cars.

_____

_____

_____

_____

c) Promoting REUSE and recycling instead of incinerating waste or sending it to landfill.

_____

_____

_____

_____

[3]